A ROOKIE BIOGRAPHY

GEORGE WASHINGTON

First President of the United States

By Carol Greene

CHILDRENS PRESS®
CHICAGO

This book is for Nicholas Kyle.

George Washington (1732-1799)

Library of Congress Cataloging-in-Publication Data

Greene, Carol.
   George Washington, first president of the United States / by Carol
Greene.
       p.   cm. — (A Rookie biography)
   Includes index.
   Summary: A simple biography of the first president of the United
States.
   ISBN 0-516-04218-1
   1. Washington, George, 1732-1799—Juvenile literature. 2. Presidents—
United States—Biography—Juvenile literature. [1. Washington, George,
1732-1799. 2. Presidents.] I. Title. II. Series: Greene, Carol. Rookie
biography.
E312.66.G74   1991
973.4'1'092—dc20
[B]
[92]   90-22195
                                                            CIP
                                                             AC

George Washington
was a real person.
He was born in 1732.
He died in 1799.
George Washington was
the first president
of the United States.
This is his story.

TABLE OF CONTENTS

The birthplace of George Washington in Virginia

Chapter 1

Just a Boy

The Washington family lived
at Ferry Farm in Virginia.
There were ten children.
But two girls died
and two older boys went
to school in England.

George and his brother Jack
did many things together.
A river ran by their farm
and they watched the boats.
They rode horses, too.
George was a fine rider.

When they studied,
George wrote his lessons
in little books.
He was good at math.
He wrote down 110 rules
about manners, too.

One rule said not to
kill fleas, ticks, or lice
in front of other people.
Another rule said not to
clean your teeth
with the tablecloth.

George wanted to go
to school in England.
But when he was 11,
his father died.
So George had to stay home.

When he was fourteen, George wanted to leave Ferry Farm
and go to sea, but his mother begged him to stay home.

George's mother, Mary Ball Washington   George's sister, Betty Washington

He didn't like that.
His mother was hard
to get along with.
George learned how
to measure land,
so he could
be a surveyor.

Mount Vernon (above) was owned
by Lawrence Washington (right).

When his older brother,
Lawrence, got married,
he moved to a farm
called Mount Vernon.
George often stayed there.

When George was 16,
he and his friend,
George William Fairfax,
went to work with surveyors
in the west.

9

George slept outdoors,
paddled a canoe,
and saw Indians dance.
He had a great time.
Soon he began to get
his own surveying jobs.

George Washington learned to use a surveyor's instrument.
Surveyors measure the land to mark out property boundaries.

Then Lawrence got sick.
George went with him to
a warm island, Barbados.
There Lawrence seemed better.

But George caught smallpox.
When he got well,
Lawrence got worse.
At last, Lawrence died.

George felt he had lost
his "best friend."
But he was a man now.
He must live his own life.

George Washington at the age of twenty-five

Chapter 2

A Soldier and a Farmer

At that time,
Virginia belonged to Great Britain.
It was a colony.
Its little army was British.
George became
part of that army.

Both Britain and France
wanted land in the Ohio Valley.
George had to go there
and spy on the French.
He did a good job.

Soon, he was head
of the whole Virginia army.
That job was too big.
George didn't know enough.
He made bad mistakes.

But the British gave
him another job.
He must lead
a general
and his army
to the French.

George Washington in his
Virginia army uniform

Washington (center) helped the British fight the French.

George knew the army
should fight in the woods,
not in open places.
He told the general.
But the general didn't listen.
Many men were killed.

Washington (on the white horse) raises his hat as his soldiers
raise the British flag over Fort Duquesne in Pennsylvania,
after the French gave up the fort.

George almost died, too.
But he got home and
people called him a hero.

He fought with the British
against the French
for three long, hard years.
When he knew for sure
the British would win,
he quit the army.

George had Lawrence's house at Mount Vernon. Now he would be a farmer.

He got married, too. Martha Custis was a widow with two small children, Patsy and Jackie. Everybody liked Martha.

Young Martha Custis (above). George meets Martha and her children (below).

View of Mount Vernon as it looks today

George worked hard.
He learned ways
to use his land better.
He bought more land.
He made the house bigger.

The Washingtons
had fun, too.
They gave parties
and they went
to parties. They
went to plays.
George liked
puppet shows.

The Washingtons at a ball—
a formal dancing party

But as time went by,
George kept thinking
about his country.
At last he decided.
America should not belong
to Great Britain anymore.

Chapter 3

The Fight for Freedom

Many other people
shared George's feelings.
Britain made the colonies
pay a lot of taxes.
But the colonies had
no power in government.

Colonists burned tax stamps. They were protesting the
right of the English king and government to tax them.

Patriots (above and top right) dressed up as Indians and dumped a shipment of British tea into Boston Harbor. English soldiers in Boston (bottom right) often fought the American colonists.

In 1773, people in Boston
threw British tea
into the harbor.
The British army
took over the city.

In 1774, the colonies
held a meeting.
George spoke for Virginia.
He hoped there
would be no war.
But things got worse.

By 1775, fighting
had already started.
The colonies met again.
They made George
commander in chief
of the American army.

Washington reviews the American army.

That was a huge job.
George had to get
food, clothes, and pay
for his soldiers.
Most had been farmers.
George trained them to fight.

In 1776, George's army
drove the British
out of Boston.
They won a battle
at Trenton,
New Jersey, too.

George Washington at Boston
Harbor (above) and receiving
the surrender of the British
commander at Trenton, New Jersey (below)

Left: Colonial leaders take down the king's arms over the door to the Supreme Court room in Independence Hall, Philadelphia. Above: The Declaration of Independence was written by a committee that included Benjamin Franklin (left) and Thomas Jefferson (seated, holding paper).

That same year,
American leaders wrote the
Declaration of Independence.
It said America was free.
The army went on
fighting for that freedom.

They had bad times.
But the winter of
1777-1778 was the worst.
George stayed with his men at
Valley Forge, Pennsylvania.

At first they lived
in tents in the snow.
They had almost no
clothes or blankets.
Some had no shoes.

When they got food,
it was bad.
One soldier said
his soup had dirt
and burned leaves in it.
He'd rather eat air.

A soldier stands watch at Valley Forge (above).
George Washington's Valley Forge headquarters (below)

By the end of the bitter winter at Valley Forge,
more than 2,500 soldiers had died of sickness.

After a while,
things got
better. But
no one ever
forgot that
winter at
Valley Forge.

At the end of the war George Washington (left)
went home to his family at Mount Vernon (right).

In spring of 1778, France
decided to help America.
More fighting lay ahead.
But at last America won.
When his country was free,
George went home.

Chapter 4

President Washington

For the next few years, George
worked at Mount Vernon.
Many people visited him.
Artists painted his picture.

George and Martha had
no children together.
Patsy and Jackie had died.
But the Washingtons
adopted Jackie's children,
George and Nellie.

The Washington family at home

George Washington, standing at the desk, was the president
of the meeting that created the Constitution.

George loved being home.
But the country needed
a new government.
So in 1787, he met
with other leaders.

They wrote the rules
for the new government.
We call these rules
the Constitution.

Then, in 1789,
George was elected
the first president
of the United States.

He didn't think
he was good enough
to be president.
But he took the job.

Opposite page: George Washington's first inauguration as president
was held in New York City on April 30, 1789.

32

Left to right: Vice President John Adams with
Washington's first Cabinet—Thomas Jefferson, Henry Knox,
Edmund Randolph, and Alexander Hamilton

The new country had
many money problems.
George helped solve them.
And he watched
his country grow.

The new government met at Federal Hall in New York City.

At first, the government
met in New York City.
Then it moved to
Philadelphia, Pennsylvania.

President Washington laid the cornerstone for the new
Capitol building in Washington, D.C., in 1793.

But there were plans
to build a new capital
on the Potomac River.
Someday it would be
called Washington, D.C.

A competition was held for the design of the new Capitol building. One version (top) featured a huge weathervane. The center design won second place. But the design at the bottom was finally adopted.

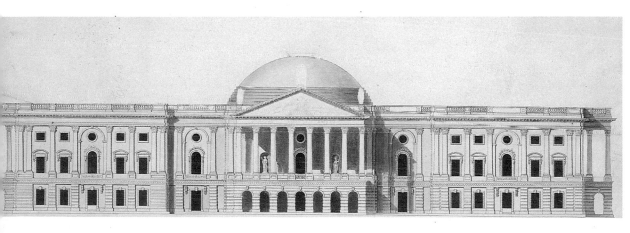

The French ambassador, Citizen Genêt, pleads with
President Washington for help against the British.

In 1792, George was
elected president again.
Great Britain and France
were still enemies.
Some people thought
America should help France.

George said no.
His country was too young.
It was growing fast.
But it needed peace.

In 1797, George's term
as president ended.
People gave speeches
and held parties
to show how much
they loved him.

That made George feel good.
But he was tired
and ready to go home.

George Washington was
happy to return
to his beloved Mount
Vernon in 1797.
He kept busy
managing the many
farms that made
up the more than
8,000 acres of
Mount Vernon.

Chapter 5

Home at Last

Back at Mount Vernon,
George worked on his
house and farm again.
He was always trying
to make them better.

Back at Mount Vernon, George could enjoy walks with his wife again.

John Adams
was the U.S.
president
from 1797
to 1801.

But France was causing
trouble for American ships.
There might be a war and
the new president,
John Adams, wanted
George to lead the U.S. army.

So George went back
to Philadelphia.
He spent months
getting the army ready.

But war never came
and George was glad.
Now he could go
home for good.

George Washington in his garden at Mount Vernon

One cold, wet day,
George rode around
his farm for five hours.
He caught a cold.
Soon he was very sick.
Doctors came, but
they couldn't help him.

On December 14, 1799,
George Washington died.

George Washington died at Mount Vernon.

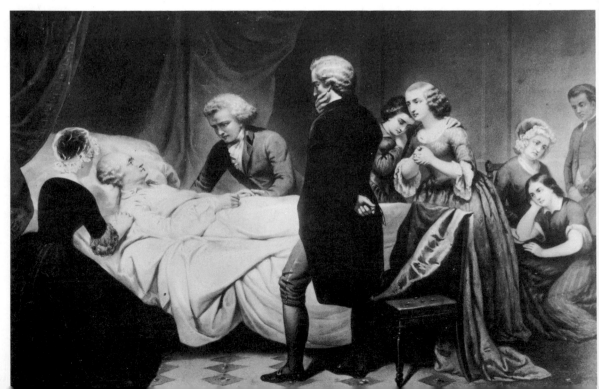

Henry Lee (above) was a leader in the war against Great Britain and a friend of George Washington.

When his soldier friend,
Henry Lee, heard that
George was dead,
he said George was:

"First in war,
first in peace,
and first in the hearts
of his countrymen."
Henry Lee was right.

Important Dates

1732   February 22—Born at Pope's Creek, Virginia, to Augustine and Mary Washington

1751   Went to Barbados with brother Lawrence

1753   Became head of part of the Virginia army

1759   Married Martha Custis

1775   Became commander in chief of American army

1787   Helped write United States Constitution

1789   Elected first president of the United States

1792   Elected to a second term as president

1799   December 14—Died at Mount Vernon, Virginia

INDEX

Page numbers in boldface type indicate illustrations.

PHOTO CREDITS

ABOUT THE AUTHOR

Carol Greene has degrees in English literature and musicology. She has worked in international exchange programs, as an editor, and as a teacher. She now lives in St. Louis, Missouri, and writes full-time. She has published more than eighty books. Others in the Rookie Biographies series include *Hans Christian Andersen, Ludwig van Beethoven, Black Elk, Elizabeth Blackwell, Daniel Boone, Christopher Columbus, Jacques Cousteau, Elizabeth the First, Benjamin Franklin, Martin Luther King, Jr., Robert E. Lee, Abraham Lincoln, John Muir, Louis Pasteur, Pocahontas, Jackie Robinson,* and *Laura Ingalls Wilder.*